discover countries

Turkey

Elaine Jackson

WAYLAND

First published in 2010 by Wayland
Reprinted in 2010 by Wayland
Copyright Wayland 2010

Wayland
Hachette Children's Books
338 Euston Road
London NW1 3BH

Wayland Australia
Level 17/207 Kent Street,
Sydney, NSW 2000

Concept design: Jason Billin
Editor: Susan Crean
Designer: Clare Nicholas
Consultants: Rob Bowden and Professor Morris Rossabi,
Distinguished Professor of History, City University of New York

Produced for Wayland by
White-Thomson Publishing Ltd

www.wtpub.co.uk
+44 (0)845 362 8240

British Library Cataloguing in Publication Data

Jackson, Elaine.
Turkey. -- (Discover countries)
1. Turkey--Juvenile literature.
I. Title II. Series
956.1'04-dc22

ISBN: 9780750259798

Printed in Malaysia
Wayland is a division of Hachette Children's Books
an Hachette UK company
www.hachette.co.uk

All data in this book was researched in 2009
and has been collected from the latest sources available at that time.

Picture credits
1, Dreamstime/Orhan Çam; 3 (top), Dreamstime/Amitai; 3 (bottom), Dreamstime/Elke Dennis; 4 (map), Stefan Chabluk; 5,
Dreamstime/Chernetskiy; 6, Dreamstime/Eddy Van Ryckeghem; 7, Dreamstime/Kobby Dagan; 8, Corbis/Owen Franken; 9, Corbis/Tolga
Bozoglu/epa; 10, Dreamstime/Amitai; 11 (top), Dreamstime/Kobby Dagan; 11 (bottom), Dreamstime/Orhan Çam; 12, Dreamstime/Kobby Dagan;
13, Walter G Allgöwer/Photolibrary; 14, Corbis/Jean-Pierre Lescourret; 15, Corbis/Kerim Okten/epa; 16, Corbis/David Lefranc/Kipa; 17,
Corbis/Patrick Ward; 18, Dreamstime/Sailorr; 19, Corbis/Adam Woolfitt; 20, Corbis/Ed Kashi; 21, Dreamstime/Sedam35; 22, Corbis/George
Steinmetz; 23 (right), Corbis/Gavin Hellier/JAI; 23 (left), Dreamstime/Elke Dennis; 24, Dreamstime/Nazira_g; 25, Corbis/Chris Hellier; 26,
Corbis/Schlegelmilch; 27, Dreamstime/Cliff Norton; 28, Nik Wheeler/Corbis; 29, Dreamstime/Benjamin Albiach Galan

Cover images, Dreamstime/Chernetskiy (left), Dreamstime/Kobby Dagan (right)

Contents

Discovering Turkey

Turkey is a rectangular-shaped country three times larger than the UK. Located between Asia and Europe, Turkey is where the countries of the East meet those of the West. For this reason, Turkey is a mixture of cultures and ideas.

Sea routes

The Turkish peninsula is surrounded on three sides by sea. Turkey also has land borders with other countries. Throughout its history, Turkey has been an important centre for trade because of its sea and land links.

Many early civilizations were established and thrived in the region. For more than a thousand years, from 330 CE to 1453, the region was the centre of the great Byzantine Empire, the eastern half of the Roman Empire.

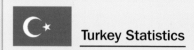

Turkey Statistics

Area: 780,580 sq km (301,384 sq miles)

Capital city: Ankara

Government type: Republican Parliamentary Democracy

Bordering countries: Armenia, Azerbaijan, Bulgaria, Georgia, Greece, Iran, Iraq, Syria

Currency: Turkish lira

Language: Turkish, Kurdish, other minority languages.

The birth of modern Turkey

At the height of its power in the sixteenth and seventeenth centuries, the Ottoman Empire covered Anatolia (modern Turkey), enormous areas of south-eastern Europe, parts of the Middle East and parts of North Africa. During the First World War (1914-1918), the Ottoman Empire fought on the side of the Germans. The war brought about the end of the empire.

The Turks, led by Mustafa Kemal, fought for independence from the Allied Powers and on 2 October 1923, Turkey was declared a republic. Mustafa Kemal was elected the first president and Ankara became capital. Kemal became known as Ataturk, or 'father of the Turks'. Until his death in 1938, Kemal worked to make Turkey into a modern country.

Turkey today

Since 1938, Turkey has continued to modernise. Turkey's economy is slowly moving away from relying on agriculture and heavy industry to a mix of services and a variety of newer industries. Good education for all Turkish citizens is seen as a priority if the country is to become strong and prosperous.

DID YOU KNOW?
Istanbul is the only city in the world located on two continents: Europe and Asia. The city was once the capital of the Roman, Byzantine and Ottoman empires.

⬧ Kocatepe Mosque was built between 1967 and 1987. It is the largest mosque in Ankara, Turkey's capital city.

Landscape and climate

Turkey has many different landscapes and climates. Along the coast are narrow strips of flat, fertile land. Inland the country is dominated by a large, high, central plateau. High, rugged mountains are found in the eastern part of Turkey.

Pamukkale, in the valley of River Menderes, is an area of sparkling white waterfalls and pools. Warm calcium-rich mineral water once flowed over cliffs and as it cooled it formed this unique natural landscape.

Mountains and earthquakes

Mount Ararat is the highest peak in Turkey. Lake Van, at 3,173 sq km (1,225 sq miles), is the largest lake. They are both located in eastern Turkey. The area also includes a number of inactive volcanoes and the source of two major rivers – the Euphrates and Tigris.

Turkey is prone to severe earthquakes, which can cause widespread destruction and death. The Kocaeli earthquake in August 1999 resulted in 17,480 deaths and 66,000 destroyed or heavily damaged houses.

Central plateau

In the middle of Turkey is the large Anatolian Plateau. The land rises in height from west to east, up to 1,200 m (4,000 ft). Steppe lands cover the central and eastern parts of the plateau. They are bare, bleak and uncultivated.

Facts at a glance

Land area: 770,760 sq km (297,592 sq miles)

Water area: 9,820 sq km (3,792 sq miles)

Highest point: Mount Ararat 5,166 m (16,949 ft)

Lowest point: Mediterranean Sea 0 m (0 ft)

Longest river: Euphrates 2,800 km (1,740 miles)

Coastline: 7,200 km (4,474 miles)

Coastal areas

Turkey's Mediterranean coast is dominated by the Taurus Mountains. They rise immediately from the coastline and reach up to 3,000 metres (10,000 ft). The Aegean coastal area has large, fertile plains and high mountain ranges that lie from east to west. Mountains line Turkey's north coast, too.

Climate

Turkey's climate is linked closely to the mountains that run alongside its coasts. The Marmara, Aegean and Mediterranean coasts enjoy a typical Mediterranean climate of hot, dry summers and mild, wet winters.

The Black Sea region has a moderate climate with warm summers, mild winters and heavier rainfall than the other regions. The mountains close to the coast prevent this Mediterranean and moderate climate extending inland, so central and eastern Anatolia experience a continental climate of extremes. Summers there are hot and dry, while the winters are very cold and snowy.

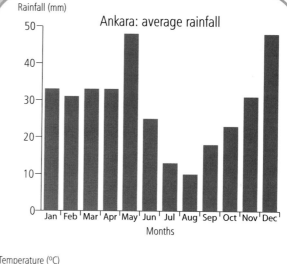

DID YOU KNOW?

According to legend, when the floodwaters went down, Noah's Ark came to a rest on Mount Ararat in eastern Turkey.

▼ Cappadocia's fairy chimneys, in central Turkey, are cones made of volcanic rocks and ash with a cap of more resistant rock. Continual erosion by the heat, frost, wind and rain has created this landscape.

Population and health

In 1950 Turkey had a population of about 21 million. By 2009 the population had increased to nearly 77 million people. The country is facing many challenges in providing health care and education for a growing number of people, particularly those who are elderly.

A growing population

Turkey has a young age structure, with children and young people making up most of Turkey's population. Only 6 per cent of Turkey's population is over the age of 65.

Even though Turkey's birth rate has more than halved since 1975, the population is still likely to be over 100 million by the year 2027. This is because the number of babies dying in infancy is declining and people are living longer.

Health and well-being

Health care in Turkey is better compared to the past but has still not reached the expected quality for a developed country, particularly in rural areas. The major causes of death in the adult population are heart disease, stroke, lung disease and cancer. Lung cancer is the most common type of cancer in Turkey due to widespread cigarette smoking. More than half of Turkish people smoke.

> **Facts at a glance**
>
> **Total population:**
> 76.8 million
>
> **Life expectancy at birth:**
> 72 years
>
> **Children dying before the age of five:** 2.9 %
>
> **Ethnic composition:** Turkish 65.1%; Kurdish 18.9%; Crimean Tatar 7.2%; Arab 1.8%; Azerbaijani 1.0%; Yoruk 1.0%; other 5.0%.

▶ About half of Turkey's population is under 25 years old, and more than 25 per cent is below the age of 15.

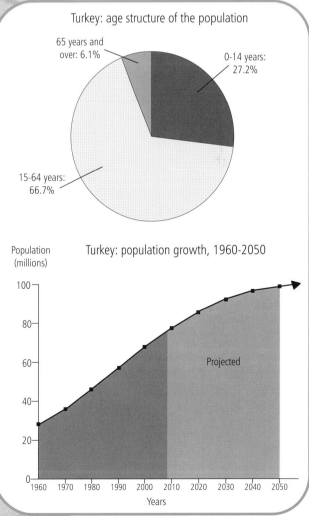
A health official wears a mask at Ataturk Airport in Istanbul. Officials worked to reduce the spread of swine flu in 2009.

Kurds in Turkey

The Kurds, the largest minority group in Turkey, lived for hundreds of years in the eastern mountains and uplands where Turkey, Iraq and Iran meet, in an area known as Kurdistan.

After the First World War, the Kurdistan region was broken up and divided between Turkey, Iraq and Iran. Kurds living in Turkey were expected to learn Turkish and to abandon their Kurdish identity, customs and traditions. The Kurds have felt pressured to conform to Turkish customs and this sometimes leads to violent clashes between Kurds and Turks.

A changing population

Since the 1960s, large numbers of people have been leaving Turkey to live and work in western European countries, particularly Germany. However, the Turkish population is not falling. Wars in neighbouring countries such as Iraq and Afghanistan have led to an increase in migrants into Turkey, while others travel through Turkey on their way to Europe. These people from war-ridden countries are seeking safety and a better lifestyle.

Turkey: age structure of the population

- 65 years and over: 6.1%
- 0-14 years: 27.2%
- 15-64 years: 66.7%

Turkey: population growth, 1960-2050

Population (millions)

Projected

Years

Settlements and living

During the past 50 years, Turkey has seen a mass movement of people from the countryside to towns and cities. People have left the villages due to high unemployment and underemployment. They move to urban areas, searching for jobs where they can earn more money.

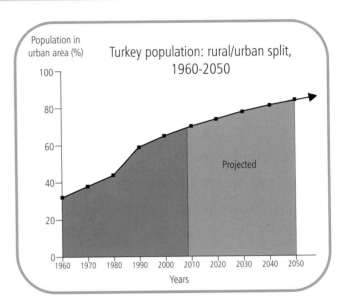

Turkey population: rural/urban split, 1960-2050

Population in urban area (%)

Projected

Years

Urban populations

About one-quarter of Turkey's population lives in the country's three largest cities: Istanbul, Ankara and Izmir. The concentration of people in a few big cities has resulted in serious problems, such as congestion, poor air and water quality and poor living conditions.

City life

There are six cities in Turkey with populations of more than one million – Istanbul, Ankara, Izmir, Bursa, Adana and Gaziantep. With more than 10 million people, Istanbul is by far the largest city.

Facts at a glance

Urban population: 69% (53 million)

Rural population: 31% (23.8 million)

Population of largest city: 10.1 million (Istanbul)

Istanbul, the largest city in Turkey, has been established for thousands of years.

▶ From the old historic centre of Ankara, the city spreads out into large, urban areas of modern apartment buildings mixed with green spaces, universities and hotels.

In city centres, high-rise office buildings, luxury hotels and fashionable shopping areas sit side by side with mosques and traditional markets and bazaars. Modernisation of cities has resulted in the building of many flats and apartments.

Settlements on the outskirts of big cities are often the first stop for migrants moving to the city from the countryside. Known as *gecekondus*, a Turkish word meaning 'thrown up overnight', these are neighbourhoods of temporary houses. These areas often have no electricity, water, drains and rubbish collection. *Gecekondus* are gradually being replaced with modern blocks of flats and apartments.

Village life

Rural areas, especially in the east, are some of the poorest areas in the country. However, in last few decades, village life has improved. Eighty five per cent of the villages have electric power and villages have become less isolated due to better communications, including the widespread use of mobile phones.

▶ There are about 45,000 villages in Turkey. Most villagers work on the land and depend on farming for their livelihood.

Family life

The family is important in Turkish society and is at the heart of daily life. Members of the extended family usually live near one another and provide help and support.

Marriage and families

Most Turkish adults get married and have children. The average age for marriage is 24 for women and 26 for men. Turkey's divorce rate is one of the lowest in the world, and single-parent families are rare.

Turkish weddings are an important part of the culture. Traditional celebrations include applying henna on the bride's hands before the wedding day, planting a flag, exchanging gifts between two families and lots of music, singing and dancing.

▼ Turkish music and traditional folk dances are part of Turkish wedding ceremonies. This celebration includes a two-piece band made up of a *zurna* (a wooden instrument a little like a clarinet) and a large drum.

Family roles

In rural areas, the father, as head of the family, is responsible for earning the money on which the whole family lives. His wife and other female members of the extended family generally look after the home, bringing up the children and doing unpaid work on the farm. In urban areas, more women work outside the home.

Warmth and generosity

Hospitality is an integral part of Turkish culture. Rather than going out, relatives, close friends and neighbours often visit each others' homes.

Turkish people are very friendly and go to great lengths to make their guests feel comfortable. Visitors are always invited in and offered something to drink and eat. Being invited for dinner with a Turkish family is a huge honour.

Shoes are taken off when entering a Turkish home, as Turks pride themselves on the cleanliness of their homes. Often, indoor shoes or slippers are provided for guests to wear. A Turkish meal is an elaborate affair. The table will be overflowing with delicious home-cooked food. It is good manners to try a bit of everything.

DID YOU KNOW?
At mealtimes, food is placed on a low table or on the floor. This is because Turkish people believe that it is healthier to eat when sitting on the floor.

Facts at a glance

Average children per childbearing woman:
2.2 children

Average household size:
4.1 people

A Turkish grandmother poses with her daughter and grandsons in front of the family home in Urfa, Turkey.

Religion and beliefs

Turkey has no state or official religion and separates religion from government. The Turkish attitude towards religion is one of tolerance and openness to different cultures and new ideas. However, 99.8 per cent of Turkey's population is Muslim, making Turkey the only mainly Muslim country in the world that has no state religion.

Centre for religion

The history of three of the world's major religions – Judaism, Christianity and Islam – is closely linked with the history of Turkey. There is evidence of a Jewish community from the fourth century BCE in Turkey. For Christians, the area is rich in Biblical history. Many Old and New Testament stories happened in Turkey. In the eleventh century, Islam spread along the Mediterranean coast and into Turkey.

Islam in Turkey

The majority of Muslims in Turkey are Sunni Muslims. Sunni Muslims believe that new leaders of the Islamic faith should be elected. The other group of Muslims is Shia Muslims. They think that leaders should come from a line of Imams, who they believe have been appointed by Muhammad.

Some Turkish Sunni Muslims practice Sufism, a mystical form of Islam. Sufi Muslims perform a dance called Sema, often also known as the dance of the whirling dervishes. The dervishes, dressed in long white dresses, whirl around while chanting Islamic poetry.

The dance of the whirling dervishes has been performed for more than 700 years. Dervish means 'doorway', believed to represent the entrance from the material world to the spiritual, heavenly world.

Celebrations

Various Muslim festivals take place in Turkey. At the end of the holy month of Ramadan, a three-day festival known in Turkey as Seker Bayrami, or Candy Festival, takes place. Elaborate desserts are prepared and children visit door to door, asking for sweets. *Lokma* (deep-fried batter in syrup) and *locum* (Turkish delight), are given to children.

Children's Day

Children are very important in Turkey. Ataturk loved children and he often said: 'Children are a new beginning of tomorrow.' He dedicated 23 April to the children of the nation. Today this is celebrated as Children's Day as well as the date when the Republic of Turkey was founded. On this day there is no school, so children enjoy the day by celebrating. There are ceremonies, performances and parades.

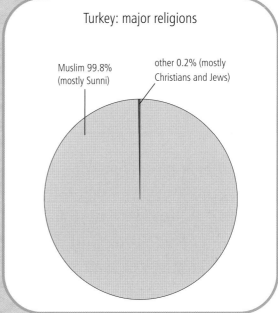

Turkey: major religions

Muslim 99.8% (mostly Sunni)

other 0.2% (mostly Christians and Jews)

▼ Turkey emphasises the love of children and hope for their future by holding a national holiday for them. Turkish flags are sold and flown on National Sovereignty and Children's Day.

DID YOU KNOW? On Children's Day, a child is placed in every government position from president to mayor. They discuss children's issues and sign orders relating to educational and environmental policies.

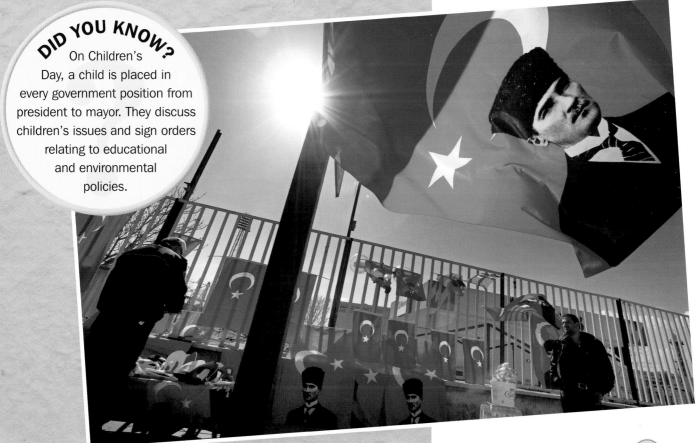

Education and learning

All Turkish children have the right to a free education. Schools work hard to ensure that every child acquires the basic knowledge, skills, behaviour and habits to become a good citizen and that each child is ready for the next stage in their life.

It's the law

Over the last decade, education has been made a national priority. All Turkish children between the ages of 7 and 14 are entitled to attend primary school for eight years. Attendance in primary school was made compulsory in 1997, however, enforcing attendance is challenging. Children leave primary school with a Primary Education certificate.

The school age population of Turkey is very large. Often there are not enough schools and teachers to cope, so the school day is divided into two sessions. Children either attend in the morning or in the afternoon.

Facts at a glance

Children in primary school:
Male 93%, Female 89%

Children in secondary school:
Male 74%, Female 64%

Literacy rate (over 15 years):
87.4%

🔻 Since 1923, Turkish pupils have worn school uniforms. This policy is changing in 2010, however, and students will wear their own clothes to school.

Classes can have up to 40 students. In some rural areas where there are not enough teachers, class sizes are even larger. A special feature of Turkish primary schools is that the same teacher teaches the same children throughout their eight years of school.

Secondary school

Three years of secondary education are free in Turkey. This has led to a significant increase in adult literacy in Turkey. However, school attendance beyond the primary level has never been required.

Many families, especially in rural areas, discourage their daughters from going to school after the age of 13 or 14. Many of them believe that it is more important for boys to be educated than girls. They think and that girls should work in the home and do not have to be educated to do so.

Universities

Entrance to Turkish universities is by entrance examination. In 2008, there were 127 universities in Turkey. About one-third of these were only established after 2006. Universities provide either two or four years of education for undergraduate students. In 2008, there were about 1.2 million undergraduates in Turkish universities.

▼ Istanbul University is the oldest university in Turkey. It was founded in 1453, and was one of the first 10 universities in Europe.

Employment and economy

Over the last 50 years, Turkey has changed from a farming to a manufacturing economy. However, farming is still important to many people. It accounts for nearly 30 per cent of employment.

Goods and services

Today, almost 63 per cent of Turkey's income is generated by service industries such as banking, insurance, tourism, hotels and restaurants. Tourism is a growing part of the service industry. It makes up 4 per cent of the country's income.

Manufacturing generates a further 28.6 per cent of Turkey's income, with textiles and clothing being the largest industrial sector in Turkey. The textile and clothing industry employs about one-third of the people who work in factories in Turkey. The automotive and electronics industries are rising in significance and produce key exports for Turkey.

Facts at a glance

Contributions to GDP:
agriculture: 8.5%
industry: 28.6%
services: 62.9%

Labour force:
agriculture: 29.5%
industry: 24.7%
services: 45.8%

Female labour force:
26.5% of total

Unemployment rate: 7.9%

⬤ Long, sandy beaches, warm seas, welcoming hospitality and good food ensure tourists enjoy their holidays in Turkey.

Employment problems

Turkey has a large labour force of more than 23 million people. However, along with Spain, Turkey has the highest unemployment rate in Europe. In addition, only 26.5 per cent of the labour force in Turkey is made up of women, which is less than half the EU average.

Turkey depends on other countries to buy the goods it makes. The global economic crisis of 2008-2009 resulted in falling demand for Turkish-made goods. Factories producing goods for foreign markets have cut back on production levels in line with shrinking markets. The slowdown in the Turkish economy means that it is especially difficult for young people to find jobs because they are less experienced.

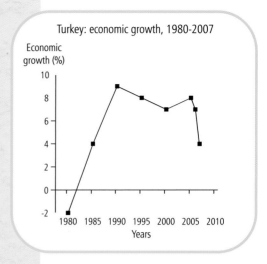

Turkey: economic growth, 1980-2007

◀ Women carpet weavers work in a factory in Istanbul. Only about one in four Turkish women has a job working outside the home.

DID YOU KNOW?

More than one million Turks work abroad. They help the Turkish economy by sending money home to their families.

Industry and trade

Turkey is ideally situated for trading routes and markets in Europe, the Middle East and Central Asia. For this reason, it has always been a centre for trade.

Natural resources

Turkey has a rich supply of minerals. Around 60 different minerals are currently produced in Turkey. Other natural resources include coal, iron ore, copper and gold.

Turkey has enormous potential to develop hydroelectric power by building dams along its many rivers. This renewable source of energy does not produce waste or pollution. However, dams on some rivers have caused some tensions between Turkey and its neighbours, Syria and Iraq.

The Ataturk Dam on the Euphrates River is the largest dam in Turkey. It provides electricity and irrigation to south-eastern Turkey.

As a desert country, Syria relies heavily on the River Euphrates. Being downstream of the Turkish dams on the River Euphrates, Syria is concerned about the flow of the water being disrupted.

Turkey also produces oil, but its level of production is not enough to make the country self-sufficient. Turkey has a central location when it comes to oil. It links, by pipeline, the major oil-producing areas in the Middle East and the Caspian Sea with Europe.

Imports and exports

Turkey's main trade partners are Germany, Italy, France, Russia, China and the USA. Some of the goods Turkey exports include textiles, iron, steel, leather goods, chemicals and machinery. The cost of Turkey's imports far exceeds the amount it makes from its exports.

Turkey is one of the leading shipbuilding nations. In 2007 the country ranked fourth in the world in terms of the number of ships ordered, and also fourth in the world in terms of the number of luxury yachts ordered. Turkey has maintained this position since 1992.

⬤ The port at Izmir is situated on the shores of the Aegean Sea. It is a major commercial and military sea port and the biggest container port in Turkey.

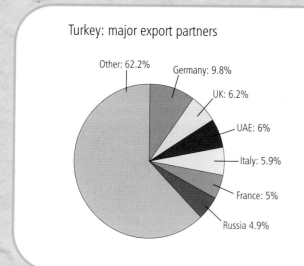

Turkey: major export partners

Other: 62.2%
Germany: 9.8%
UK: 6.2%
UAE: 6%
Italy: 5.9%
France: 5%
Russia 4.9%

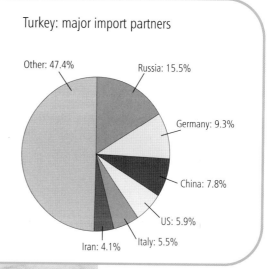

Turkey: major import partners

Other: 47.4%
Russia: 15.5%
Germany: 9.3%
China: 7.8%
US: 5.9%
Italy: 5.5%
Iran: 4.1%

Farming and food

Turkey, because of its land, climate and hard-working farmers, is one of few countries in the world that produces enough food to feed all its people.

Commercial crops

A wide range of crops can be grown in Turkey because of the different climates throughout the land. This has allowed the country to become a major producer and exporter of agricultural products. The country's main export markets are the EU and the USA, to which Turkey exports dried fruit and nuts, cotton and tobacco.

Turkey is the world's largest producer of hazelnuts, cherries and apricots. It ranks highly in the production of other fruits and vegetables including watermelons, cucumbers, tomatoes and aubergines.

Turkey is the leading world producer of apricots. Here, women split the apricots and put them out to dry. They will later be made into jam.

The major industrial crops produced in Turkey are cotton, tobacco and sugar beets. The country is one of the world's largest cotton growers. Turkey's tobacco production makes up 4 per cent of global production, placing Turkey fifth after China, India, the USA and Brazil.

Food and diet

In Turkey, meat usually means lamb, the main ingredient to the country's most popular national dish, the kebab (skewered grilled meat). Aubergines are a popular vegetable in Turkey, followed by courgettes and then beans, artichokes and cabbages.

Lokum (Turkish delight) is made from cooking melted sugar and cornflour. Walnuts, nuts and pistachios are used for filling. It is produced in different colours and aromas.

DID YOU KNOW?
Turkish coffee is a thick brew served hot from a special coffee pot and drunk from small cups. It is served after nearly every meal and has six levels of sweetness, ranging from very sweet to bitter.

▼ *Yaprak dolma* is a dish of vine leaves stuffed with ground meat or seasoned rice.

▶ The Sultanahmet area of Istanbul is very popular in the summer for outdoor dining.

Around major urban areas, roads are paved and in good condition. However, in rural areas, they are not always well maintained. However, roads are necessary for most types of transport in Turkey.

Types of transport

Coaches and buses run frequent services between Turkish cities. In Turkey, coaches are generally faster than trains. The journey from Istanbul to Ankara takes about six hours. By rail, the same journey can take up to 10 hours. Turkish railways and trains are old and relatively slow, though they do connect Turkey's major cities.

The journey from Istanbul to Ankara takes only 45 minutes by air. Internal flights also connect major cities. They are convenient, reasonably priced and quicker than travelling by road or rail. The principal airports for international scheduled flights are located in seven cities, including Istanbul, Ankara and Izmir.

Facts at a glance

Total roads: 426,951 km (265,295 miles)

Paved roads: n/a

Railways: 8,697 km (5,404 miles)

Major airports: 48

Major ports: 6

As a big metropolis, with around 14 million inhabitants, Istanbul has traffic congestion problems. Every day, morning and evening rush hours lead to traffic jams.

City Travel

In cities and large towns, local bus services are generally reliable, modern and easy to use. Taxis are numerous. A *dolmus* (pronounced dohl-moosh) is a shared taxi or minibus which follows specific routes within large cities, suburbs and to neighbouring towns. *Dolmus* means 'filled', which is what the vehicle needs to be before it departs.

Communication

Mobile phones have made communication much easier in Turkey and more people are now using the Internet, too. From 2001 to 2006, the use of mobile phones nearly tripled in Turkey and the number of citizens with Internet access increased by more than five times. Turkey has the eleventh-largest population of Internet users worldwide.

🔺 Istanbul has a fleet of modern and efficient trams as well as more traditional trams, such as the one shown here.

Turkey: Internet and mobile phone use, 1995-2007

Millions

- Mobile phones in use
- Internet subscribers

Years: 1995, 2000, 2005, 2010

Leisure and tourism

The variety and beauty of Turkey's landscapes attracts tourists to its beaches, mountains, plains and valleys. Tourist attractions range from rich archaeological and historical sites to seaside and spa resorts.

Tourism

The Turkish tourism industry has experienced incredible growth over the past few years. Cheaper and more frequent flights to and from other European countries have made a big difference. During 2008, Turkey received more than 26 million international tourists. The country has become a popular tourist destination for many Europeans.

However, 40 per cent of Turkey's own population never goes on holiday. Turks who do go on holiday tend to go the Turkish coastal areas. If they spend their holiday abroad, Turks generally prefer Italy or the South of France. However, over the last 10 years, the Adriatic coast of Croatia has become a popular summer destinations for Turks.

A sporting nation

The most popular sport in Turkey, for both spectators and participants, is football. Some clubs, such as Galatasaray and Fenerbahçe, are located in Istanbul.

The Turkish Grand Prix is a favourite fixture for Formula 1 fans around the world. In addition to boosting tourism, the Turkish Grand Prix helps to promote the automotive industry in Turkey.

Racing cars on the Turkish Grand Prix circuit run in an anti-clockwise direction. This is only the third race on the F1 Grand Prix calendar to do so.

A variety of other sports, including volleyball, basketball, wrestling and swimming, are also enjoyed in Turkey.

Other spare time activities

Leisure activities in Turkey also include watching television, going to the cinema, shopping and socialising in the home or in cafés and restaurants. Turkish music is a rich blend of classical and folk music. It represents the different areas and cultural mix in Turkish society. Young people like pop music and folk music, known as *Turku*, which is often played at weddings, other celebrations and funerals.

⬤ Grease wrestling is a popular Turkish sport and every year in July, championships are held. Contestants rub olive oil into their skin to make it difficult for their opponent to hold onto them.

DID YOU KNOW?
The Grand Bazaar in Istanbul is one of the largest covered markets in the world. It has more than 58 streets with 4,000 shops selling spices, jewellery, leather, pottery and carpets.

Environment and wildlife

Turkey is rich in animal species. The fallow deer and the pheasant are native to Turkey. Mountains and national parks are populated with wildlife, such as brown bears, wild boar, lynx, wolves and hundreds of species of birds.

Problems with the environment

As the Turkish economy has grown, so has the level of pollution in the air and water. The country has had to import more oil and gas, putting the surrounding seas at greater risk of oil spills, too. Already there have been some accidents, but many are worried that a major accident will occur.

Facts at a glance

Proportion of area protected: 5.8%

Biodiversity (known species): 9,362

Threatened species: 68

▼ The first dam in Turkey was built at Kaban along the Euphrates in 1974. Since then, numerous dams have been built to generate electricity and provide fresh water.

Plants and animals

Turkey has many areas that have remained free of people, making it possible for many rare and endangered species of wildlife to live there. More than 75 per cent of the total number of plant species found in the whole of Europe grow in Turkey.

Cherries, apricots, almonds and figs all originated in Turkey. Turkish plants also include many wild relatives of important crops, such as wheat, apples, pears and apricots. Colourful flowers, such as pink oleander bushes, red anemones and poppies, grow wild on hillsides throughout Turkey.

Protecting wildlife

Turkey's Aegean and Mediterranean shores provide a place of safety for the endangered monk seals and several varieties of turtles. Turkey's efforts to protect the Loggerhead Sea Turtle have been extremely successful. After the construction of a planned luxury hotel on a beach where the turtles breed was abandoned in 2009, the area at Dalyan has become a wildlife sanctuary.

▶ Loggerhead sea turtles live in Turkey's coastal areas. They live, on average, for more than 50 years.

Glossary

Allied Powers the group of countries that fought on the same side as Great Britain during the First World War and Second World War

archaeology study of prehistoric remains

bazaar a market, often covered

civilization type of culture and society developed by a particular nation or region or in a particular period of history

climate normal weather conditions of an area

compulsory something that must be done

dependent someone who relies on another person, for example, for food or money

depopulation when people move away from an area and population decreases

economy way that trade and money are controlled by a country

endangered in danger of becoming extinct

extended family members of a family beyond mother, father and their children

export good or service that is sold to another country

extinct no longer exists

fertile good for growing crops, especially in large quantities

GDP (gross domestic product) the total value of goods and services produced by a country

habitat the place where animals and plants live and exist

hospitality the welcoming of guests

hydroelectric type of electricity produced by water power

Imam Muslim prayer leader and teacher of religion

import good or service that is bought in from another country

immigrants people who come to live in a new country

irrigation a system of ditches and channels made to provide water to dry land

landscape physical features (such as mountains, rivers and deserts) of a place

metropolis large urban area or city

migration movement of people from one place to another

mosque Muslim place of worship

Muhammad the prophet of Islam, to whom God revealed the words of the Qur'an

Muslims followers of the religion of Islam

natural resources naturally occurring things found in land, air or water which are useful to human beings

neutral not on one side or the other

peninsula land surrounded on three sides by water

plateau wide area of flat land that is high up

pollution substances that contaminate or poison, such as chemical waste

refugee person who has fled from danger or a problem

republic a system of government in which people elect officials to make decisions on their behalf

rural to do with the countryside or agriculture

secular without an official religion

self-sufficient able to provide for one's self

service industries part of the economy that provides services such as banking, insurance, tourism, hotels, restaurants and healthcare

steppe lands dry, cold grasslands

surplus amount left over

textile fabric or cloth

underemployment not employed the full amount of hours one is available to work or in a way that best uses one's abilities

urban to do with towns and town life

Topic web

**Use this topic web to explore Turkish themes
in different areas of your curriculum.**

History
Find out about Ephesus or another important historical site in Turkey. Make a poster to explain what you have found out.

Geography
Use reference books, tourist brochures, Internet and other sources of information to plan a visit to Turkey. Create a schedule that includes the places you want to visit and why.

Science
Turkey produces some electricity from hydroelectric power. List the advantages and disadvantages of producing electricity this way.

Maths
Find out how many Turkish lira there are in £1. Select five items (e.g. a bottle of water, a piece of fruit, etc) and work out how much they would cost in Turkish lira.

Turkey

ICT
Prepare a presentation of images of Turkey to show the wide variety of things there are to do on a holiday in Turkey.

Design and Technology
Design a menu for a Turkish meal. Ask an adult to help you prepare the meal. Invite a friend to your Turkish lunch.

Citizenship
Create a list of what makes a 'good' holidaymaker and what makes a 'bad' holidaymaker.

English
Write reasons why Loggerhead Sea Turtles and the beach at Dalyan need to be protected. Write the reasons as bullet points.

Further information and index

Further reading

Turkey (Eyewitness Travel Guide) by Suzanne Swan (DK Publishing, 2008)
Welcome to Turkey (Welcome to My Country) by Vimala Alexander (Franklin Watts)
Turkey (World in Focus) by Anita Ganeri (Wayland, 2007)

Web

http://news.bbc.co.uk/1/hi/world/europe/country_profiles/1022222.stm
This is the BBC's country profile of Turkey. You can find lots of background information, current news and a timeline of major events in Turkish history.

http://www.allaboutturkey.com
On this site you will find lots of information about the country of Turkey.

Index